Simon B Pocket Coloring Book

Volume II, Hearts

Color your way into love with this travel sized book of romantic hearts from acclaimed artist Simon Bull.

Take it with you to turn any quiet corner into your personal haven of creative renewal, in the air, at sea, on the road or at home.

So then, grab those colored pencils, because it's time to climb on board the love train. Choose the heart that suits your mood and settle into some downtime that will put the color back into the black and white of your day!

Enjoy.
Simon Bull

Share your masterpiece with the world!

Why not post your finished works with other
Simon Bull Coloring Book enthusiasts online? Just take a picture
and post it!

Facebook:
www.facebook.com/simonbullart

Instagram:
#simonbullcoloringbook

Twitter:
@Simon_Bull_Art

For more information on Simon Bull visit:
www.bullart.com

You can order more copies of this and other Simon Bull Coloring
Books on
Amazon.com

Our hearts lie at the center of our being. From our hearts radiate the roads, the little pathways over which we travel to the outside world. So, look after your heart, nurture it like a well watered garden and it will continually direct your steps into the way of peace.

Simon Bull

Give it Heart

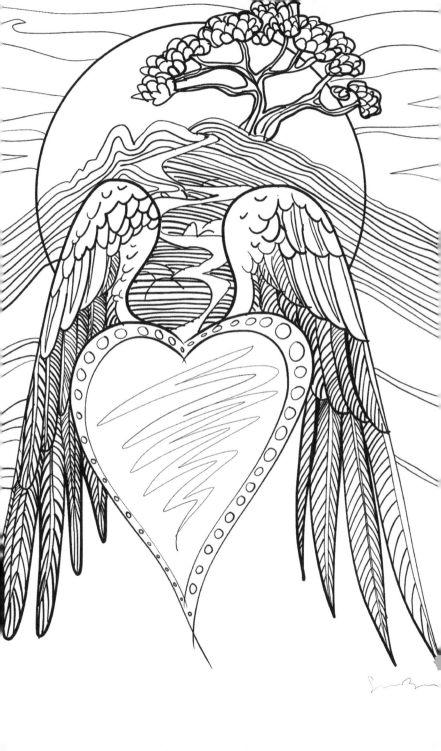

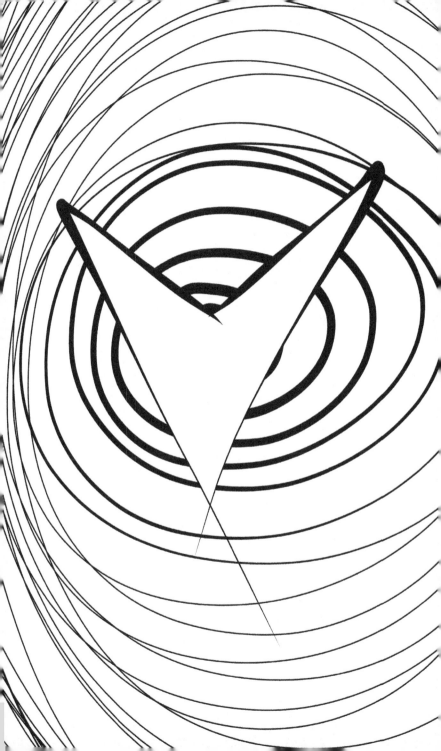

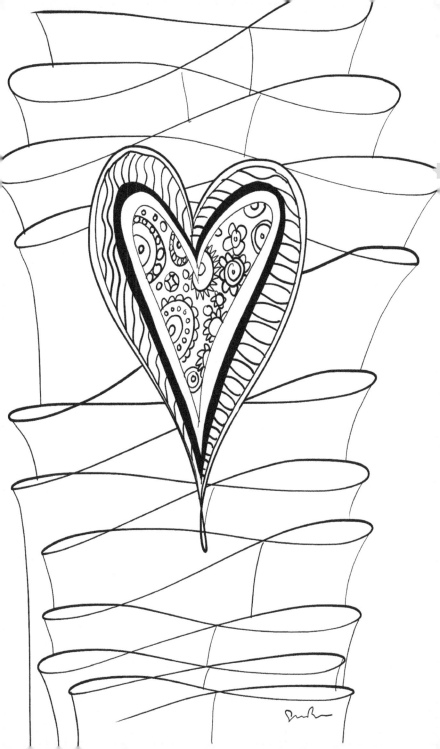

is
LOVE
THE
FINEST
THING
OF ALL?

About the artist

Simon Bull's vibrant paintings are infused with a joy and humor that celebrates all that is good in life, whether it be a simple flower, a stunning heart, a glass of wine, or the flowing lines of a saxophone.

Artist and cancer survivor, Simon learnt the hard way the importance of celebrating life's great little moments as they happen. "I wanted my paintings to lift people's spirits, to send them on their way with a smile on their face, like a shot of caffeine in the morning."

His paintings have been featured on ABC Television's Extreme Makeover Home Edition, MTV Cribs, ShopNBC and on cruise ships worldwide. They have been introduced by Randy Jackson of American Idol, unveiled by Ashley Judd among others and can be found in many collections both public and private around the world.

Career Highlights
Official Artist - Salt Lake Winter Olympics.
Official Artist - Boxing Legend Muhammad Ali.
Multiple Award Winner - 'US Limited Edition Print of The Year'. NALED
Winner - 'Artist Print Award' Best selling printmaker in Great Britain.

Simon Bull resides in California.

Made in the USA
Monee, IL
02 June 2021